# THE MOTHE

Born in New York City, Jeri Kroll has an honours degree from Smith College, a Masters from the University of Warwick (UK) and a Ph D from Columbia University. She taught in the U.S. and England before moving to Australia in 1978 where she is Associate Professor of English and Program Coordinator of Creative Writing at Flinders University.

She has published twenty previous books for adults and young people, including poetry, picture books (two Children's Book Council Notable Awards), novels and anthologies. Her first collection of poems, *Death as Mr Right*, won second prize in the Anne Elder Award. Her most recent novel for older readers (May 2004), is *Mickey's Little Book of Letters*.

Marian Cohen Kroll (aka Marian Hollis) had a career in show business as a dancer and singer before she married in 1941. Her daughter Jeri took classes at the New Dance Group Studio in New York City and performed with Jean-Leon Destiné's Afro-Haitian Dance Company. Now she events and showjumps on her horse, Petros.

By the Same Author

Poetry
*House Arrest*
*Monster Love*
*Indian Movies*
*Death as Mr. Right*

Fiction
*The Electrolux Man and Other Stories*

Young Adult Fiction
*Riding the Blues*
*Beyond Blue*
*Better Than Blue*

Older Reader Fiction
*Bruise*
*Goliath*

Chapter Book
*Fit for a Prince*

Children's Picture Books
*A Coat of Cats*
*Swamp Soup (poems)*
*What Goes With Toes?*
*Beaches*
*Sunny Faces*
*You Be the Witch*

Anthologies (co-edited)
*Tuesday Night Live: Fifteen Years of Friendly Street.* Eds. Jeri Kroll,
Barry Westburg (including a history of Friendly Street).
*Montage.* Eds. Val Driesener, Jeri Kroll, Anne-Marie Mykyta
*No. 8 Friendly Street Poetry Reader.* Eds. Robert Clark, Jeri Kroll.

# THE MOTHER WORKSHOPS
and other poems

Jeri Kroll

Five Islands Press

Published by
Five Islands Press Pty Ltd,
PO Box U34
Wollongong University 2500
FAX 02 4272 7392
email kpretty@uow.edu.au

Cover photographs of Marian Hollis by Bloom (Chicago)
Author photograph: Molten Peg Studio

National Library of Australia
Cataloguing-in-Publication Entry
Kroll, Jeri 1946–
The mother workshops
ISBN 1 74128 035 4
1. Title
A821.3

This project was assisted by the Commonwealth Government
through the Literature Board of the Australia Council, the Federal
Government's arts funding and advisory body.

In Memory of my Mother
Marian (Hollis) Cohen Kroll
Born 13 September 1911
Died 22 November 1998

And for my sister, Judith Kroll

## Acknowledgements

Poems in this collection have appeared in *Accounting, Auditing and Accountability, Among Ants, Between Bees, Another Universe: Friendly Street Poets 28, BankSA Year 2000 Writers' Competition: Winning Entries, beyond the shimmering, The Bunyip, Canadian Woman Studies, Friendly Street 22, Midday Horizon: First Choice of Australian Poets No 2, Salt 12* and *Salt 17: An International Journal of Poetry and Poetics, Southern Review, Storie, the write side/Pomeriggio/Afternoon/ten to six* (Italian/ English), *TEXT: The Journal of the Australian Association of Writing Programs, Time's Collision with the Tongue: The Newcastle Poetry Prize Anthology 2000, Voices: Journal of the National Library of Australia.*

Some poems have been broadcast by ABC Radio National's *PoeticA*. Some poems were written while the author held a residential fellowship in 2000 at Varuna Writers' Centre in NSW (Eleanor Dark Foundation).

Quotations from:

Margaret Atwood, "Circe/Mud Poems" in *You Are Happy.* Toronto: Oxford University Press, 1974.
*The Harvard Mental Health Letter*, Volume II, Number 8 (February 1995), 1.
Samuel Beckett, *How It Is.* Grove Press: New York, 1964, 7.
Jorge Luis Borges, "The South" in *Fictions*, ed. and with an introduction by Anthony Kerrigan. New York: Grove Press, 1962, 154.
Morris Lurie, *Whole Life.* Melbourne: McPhee Gribble, 1987, 177.
Adrienne Rich, "When We Dead Awaken: Writing as Re-Vision" in *Adrienne Rich's Poetry* , eds. Barbara Charlesworth Gelpi and Albert Gelpi. New York: Norton, 1975, 90-98.

# Part 1

## A Coastal Grammar

A Coastal Grammar

    I   Normanville           13

    II   Still Life with Dog and Fire    15

    III  Water to Water    16

    IV  What was the word for that fish?    18

Warning: Gale Force Winds    20

Missing the Dogs    21

Gothic Air    23

Castaways    24

Millennium Sun    25

Doing My Tax Towards Evening    26

10 Things You Can Do With Your Son's Room    27

Lying In    29

# Part 2

## The Mother Workshops

Exercise 1:   Similes    33

Exercise 2:   Exposition    34

Exercise 3:   Syntax    35

Exercise 4:   Synecdoche    37

Exercise 5:    Memoir    38

Exercise 6:    Writing to Music    45

Exercise 7:    Making Use of Errors    46

Exercise 8:    Found Poem    47

Exercise 9:    Villanelle    48

Exercise 10:    A Postmortem Workshop    49

Exercise 11:    Sonnet    53

Exercise 12:    The subject is. . .    54

Exercise 13:    Paternal Interlude    55

Exercise 14:    Wordplay    57

Exercise 15:    Factions    59

Exercise 16:    Poetry as Catharsis    62

Exercise 17:    Generational Comparisons    63

Exercise 18:    Re-Vision    66

Exercise 19:    Meditations on Food    68

Exercise 20:    Personification    71

Exercise 21:    Using Letters    73

Exercise 22:    Meditations on Objects    75

Exercise 23:    Response to Legal Jargon    78

Exercise 24:    Souvenirs    79

Exercise 25:    Coda    81

# Part 1

# A Coastal Grammar

# I  Normanville

Fleurieu Peninsula, SA

1
Wind scours this land
but we have done right by it.
Enough kikuyu roots in the sand
above the limestone reef
to keep our soil from coating city streets
or dusting the neighbour's cows
clustered about the Gothic pine
in a corner near the fence line
where our horses, bums to the wind,
ride out the storm.

2
In the wettest year we planted,
spending all our cash to spray, slash and seed.
The ground grew warm, enough to germinate,
and the rain laughed down
to win our bet with a neighbour
– a six-pack if our paddocks were green by December,
an unlikely scenario at any time.
But even though we seeded late,
phalaris and cocksfoot pushed ahead
like the dark horse at the track – 200 to 1.

We closed our eyes, held our breath,
while rain ruined weekend after weekend
for everyone in the city.  We opened one eye,
admired the crewcut on the land,
talked about kikuyu in a pastoral trance
and had no pity on our friends.
Saturday farmers, this was our one chance
to send out runners, settle in,
pretend to permanence, although that reef
still stretched unbroken to the sea.

3
Our trees, too, have taken root:
"You barely see the shed from the road," we say.
At first we planted store-bought tubes,
then germinated from local stock.
Acacia sophorae (coastal wattle) –
children of the caravan park, the nature strip,
looped with irrigation pipe,
accelerated past pine and Queensland box,
showering us with golden sprays.
We sneezed and harvested their seeds.

Our forest needs a name, our son says.
He posts his choices on the fridge:
Beachside Forest, Willis Wood.
He maps the property meticulously;
sites the shed, dam, crosscountry course,
the bore we can't afford to dig,
arena, diet paddock, future house.
Now he needs to know
where we'd like to be buried.

4
On his map you make an X  by a fence.
I don't refuse him now, I just delay,
wondering at this passion for permanence
in a child who hardly knows decay.
Our son has always battled winds and tides.
He's like the bet we made and won.
He covets names and generations.  At ten,
he plans to walk these paddocks with his children,
even though they, too, will be city-bred.
Already he sinks beneath the reef

with what he has decided to remember:
stories about how we planted forests
and bred horses, he and his gambling parents
who fertilise, under granite headstones,
this land, which remains impossibly green,
December after December.

## II Still Life with Dog and Fire

"... [for humans live] in time, in succession, while the magical
animal lives in the present, in the eternity of the instant."
                                        Jorge Luis Borges


Does age smell?  The older the dog grows
the more he smells like a labrador,
though he's  border collie and blue heeler.
His skin shows his age, mottled like a wino's.
He's allergic to fleas.  If he could talk,
 he'd sound just like my mother.
"Not bad.  But I've seen the doctor again."

 Age is one damn thing after another.
The dog copes as best he can,
but does he recall when he could run
without dragging his rear end?
Does he think in  his doggy way of limber days?
"Ah, I remember when I raced across the paddocks
 after the horses – once the filly tried to kick me."

He sleeps before the fire on a rug,
his breathing deep and even,
trusting in eternal love and gas.
I envy that oblivion.
His rhythm's like the waxing summer tide
that edges up the beach in perfect time
with firelight melting in the waves.
He doesn't seem to brood on age,
and so we don't brood with him.
His sleep forgives us all.

He lifts an eyelid as I rise
and pass to call my mother,
lowers it when I dial.
As I recite the caring catechism –
how, why, when –

feeling patience stiffen
and fail in the gloom beyond the warmth,
I lose myself in this present vision:

a young dog  curled up on a rug,
sleeping  by a never ending fire.

## III  Water to Water

> "In the late stages demented people can no longer recognize friends
> and relatives. Their speech is reduced to a few repeated phrases."
> *The Harvard Mental Health Letter* [on Alzheimer's]

My mother is floating out to sea
without buoy or boat.  She smiles as she drifts.
Light dapples in her eyes like sun on water
when rolling clouds pass over.

Almost eight years since her last visit.
We came here once to show off beach and land,
the sea she dipped a toe in.
She never saw dolphins or pelicans
that appear  like a gift of effortless sleep.

Now the sea is dolphin smooth.
Nothing worth comment breaks the skin.
I imagine her drift beyond the reef,
suddenly riding breakers.

What was the word for that fish
with the triangle fin
that looks as if it is grinning?
She scans the horizon for a hint.
Only the glint of light on her cloud-grey hair
betrays where she is.  And her unnamed fear.

Perhaps she'll meet dolphins after all
and ask for their secret:
where did that hand come from
tucked up in their sides?

I never asked if she were afraid
when she couldn't remember her grandsons' names.
I took it as given.  "You must be frightened," I said,
speaking my terror into her skin.

I stand on the winter beach at dusk.
Swells threaten the track tonight,
the dunes next year, our unbuilt house in thirty.
I'm happy to see the ocean broken,
happy she's now far enough out
to take pleasure in pure motion.

My mother has taught me a lesson without a sound.
Words wash over her now.
It doesn't matter what she's floating in.
Even the word *sea* means nothing
because she becomes it.

## IV  What was the word for that fish?

"The writer is like a foetus trying to do gymnastics."
Samuel Beckett

Shark alert on the coast last summer.
We scampered out near rocks, panting in the heat,
our insides delicious with terror.
Abandoned boogie boards teased on the tide.

At twenty, I wanted to die,
got as far as a cigarette burn on my leg.
I was a jaded coward, knew with a few drunken friends
we had nothing to live for
and talked the topic to death.
Finally I am what I planned at sixteen
when I was at peak bone mass
and totally out of control of my heart.

I still talk late at night – about building houses,
about seaweed fouling the beaches. Will the sea rise?
Yes, my neighbour and I agree,
scratching our paranoid places.
Later, asleep in our shed,
I dream of horses racing the tide.
Already it leaps up the tracks where we ride.
Deep sand's heavy going, hard on their muscles.

The track sucks me in like the judgment I vowed
I wouldn't make of myself.  And did.
My mare lathers up, all nerves,
gallops off, foam licking her heels.

In the morning, we plan the house. The council insists.
I worry about percentages and genes.
What will my son inherit? What have I?
These winter nights mind shuts early.
I can't buy the right word so settle for something like warmth.

I look like my mother the older I grow,
even the shape of my skull.
What's the basic stuff of which we are made?
Various ancient Greeks had it right:
earth, air, fire, water –
the body's 98% full.
My mother's neurons have tangled.
The inlet's clogged. Nothing flows.

It's late in the piece to change plans.
I can't be a surgeon or gymnast.
I still strongarm answers from intractable voices.
"Yes ma'am, no ma'am," they dissemble.
"Have you said what you mean?"
Not yet. Not yet.

The beach curls out of sight like a question mark.
Sea is deceptively calm.
Some days it all seems simple.
Words are like grains of sand.
You scoop a beachful, sift it through your fingers.
You make a choice.

And there's always the sea to stare at
till the glare makes everything merge,
you forget grains of sand
were anything other than grains
and waves just moon-mad water.

I will sift and stare till evening
till the word *words*
means nothing
as I become them.

# Warning: Gale Force Winds

Fleurieu Peninsula

The summer poem has just been blown away.

The poem glistening with sweat, dozing on a chaise.
The poem jogging down a deserted beach.
The poem surging like an exultant pup
in and out of the waves.

Because wind around here is worse than a parent
who's always right,
more fierce than a tyrant most days on the coast,
shouting everyone down,
blasting words into syllables, keening vowels.
Wind forces trees into disabled postures,
licks dusty paddocks,
coughs topsoil over the bay.

Frustrator of kids, coating ice blocks with sand,
despoiler of rose bed harmonies,
hider of toys behind water tanks,
breaker of pots, loser of keys,
lord of the one left gardening glove
before whom we sprint to rescue the wash
and calm the scatty cat.

On these end-of-the-world days,
wind gusts through the skull without warning
as nightmares that refuse to back down in the light.
We know there's a message somewhere
echoing in our bones:
I am the master's voice.
Make sense of me if you dare.

# Missing the Dogs

1

Alone on the south coast in a dogless house,
I know I am no island.
My hand dangles useless at my side;
no velvet heads to stroke.
Reduced to talking to myself
I contemplate this state of being
without dogs – companions, playmates, guards,
all-around fussy shadows.

The autumn chill sniffs up my spine. The truth?
I miss their undiluted joy,
the absolute despair that switches on
with the car's engine. I drive off like a star,
half loving, half embarrassed at the fuss.

So am I really leader of the pack,
or has the pack been leading me?
Do dreams that make paws twitch
include a vision of me in slow mo,
floating down the lawn,
arms full of roasted chickens?

Dogs feed our illusions.
You toss a ball, they fetch your self-esteem,
lay it at your feet.
They never notice wrinkles, grey or fat.
This symbiosis comes from needy love.

2

The Dark Ages were enlightened about dogs.
Consider the knight's sarcophagus.
Fidelity, thy name is Fang,
the cushion for thy master's feet.

Even in our own benighted times
my dogs remain my champions.
I'm sure they'd nip St Peter's heels
as well as mine to herd me into heaven,
yelping my arrival to the angels.

"Make way, make way. This is she,
dispenser of all good.
Make ready an honoured seat –
preferably by a fire,
with a sheepskin rug before,
so we can turn three times around
and settle at her feet."

## Gothic Air

I'm being dismembered by mail.
Bits of me fly across the Pacific
packed in plastic bubbles, cotton, foam,
smothered by layers of home
so my past doesn't stain the clouds,
only a hint of pink on their virginal sheen.
And the dozy Customs man won't even blink
at the neat brown parcels, wavy print.

My mother is mailing me back.

Trophies, report cards and degrees
recycle across the seas.
Then the college pictures.
There I'm thin, my hip bones point like fingers –
*Gaunt is Good* – my anorexic stage.

A week later, salvage starts again.
In camp photos I'm a well-fed ten,
smiling for all I am worth –
two dollars fifty – a sign of wealth
when I  secreted coins in a sock,
which mother kindly encloses (and has washed).

A lock of baby hair, two bronzed shoes,
three teeth, sharp as her purpose.
What have I done to deserve this?
I have grown up.  I have grown old.

# Castaways

Upstaging Tom Hanks

Sea spat us out on a shore
flat as a child star's chest.
We watched the yacht sink
against a magnificent backdrop –
Campari straight up with a lemon twist.

We shivered in the wind
that blew our holiday off course.
We almost smiled, knowing we finally deserved
to be depressed. After all,
the Valium, Prozac and Coke
had gone down with the ship.

On the sand, we postmortemed the disaster.
Who was supposed to be steering?
Had anyone checked on the weather?
Had anyone seen the reef,
waiting to scar like a marital tiff?
Where in hell were we
besides somewhere north of Australia?

We squabbled over three chocolates,
unstuck from the deck hand's pocket,
two washed-up bottles of tonic,
a blanket, the colour of hemp,
drying on a shapely leg of driftwood.

Recriminations materialised in the dusk
one by one with the stars.
The air held us moistly together.
Already we hated each other –
our voices, our swollen eyes,
our smell of futility,
our worries over what we'd left undone.

This was day one.

# Millennium Sun

The century strutted out like a supermodel,
thrust a hip, took a bow,
whirled back to life as usual –
a civilisation still in love with youth:

the Venus de Milo with arms,
tan from exotic locations,
and screen muscle flexing before the kill.

Only the sun stands up for age,
burns us back to size.
A decade or two makes all the difference.

"You've hardly changed" – the phrase
we all hope to boil down to,
the cream that smooths the truth around the eyes.

Ah, but sun, you have what we want.
Vigorous as a Biblical patriarch,
nothing filters your power
in this birthslick millennium.

Cosmetic surgeons can't compete.
We're all on a global plan,
never miss a treatment.

"Brightness falls through the air;
who will die young and fair"?
Ozone thins as species on the ground.

Scan the treeless horizons
where farmers' childhoods erode
and the shadow of the hanged man
swirls in a yellow wind gritty with hope.

Only the sand's skin,
smooth as a face in death,
relaxes the surface of the world.

Time to sleep.

## Doing My Tax Towards Evening

Cool skin, cool head, cool screen –
humming the cyberspace blues.
Cool bills, paid long ago,
rustling in piles, tempting me to burn.

My back's stiff as an accountant's tool.
He riseth up in the morning,
cracks the whip and black-clad numbers obey.
I sin the sin of envy.

I can't remember if there was a sky
last time I looked. I look.
It's the slack-jawed grey
of an idiot fog that remembers nothing.

That's autumn all over today.
I wish for the release of smoke,
slips of paper hissing goodbye to ink,
a vandal wind with no respect for law

to whip up flames and cauterise
me as well as the sky.
Ashes – many happy returns
of the end of the day.

# Ten Things You Can Do With Your Son's Room Now That He's Left Home

1. Leave his door and window open
to ventilate the house
because no one's there to curse
the invasion of privacy.

2. Meditate on his chair
although bits of home-grown weed
stick to your pants and beer
exhales from the lumpy seat.

3. Convert it to a gym
though he took one of the weights.
Will you overdevelop an arm
or double your exercise time?

4. Store the Everest of cans,
cardboard, bags and glass.
Then cash the bottles in
and keep the money.

5. Use the closet for his father's clothes
since he won't be borrowing them.
Did he take those buttery leather shoes
and that wicked black silk shirt?

6. Prop yourself against the wall,
close your eyes and listen to music.
But he's taken the CD player
and you no longer need to chill out.

7. Hide your duty-free gin
and expensive chardonnay.
But since he and his mates have gone
the wine rack is safe again.

8.  Retire to read in comfort
on his untouched single bed.
But the ghost of his smaller body
leans close as you turn the pages.

9.  Retreat from a fight with his father –
though now you don't squabble about him
the war seems to be over.
Why doesn't it feel like peace?

10.  Feel through midnight's dark
past dreaming dogs to his room.
Steal in and stand by the bed,
listening to no one breathe.

# Lying In

Sparrows snip at the mellow light.
Sun falls in triangles on the rug.
The day adds to itself,
then divides into useful sections:

a recycling truck, a car gunning to work,
a whistler dropping leaflets,
while all along the verandah,
three cats complain for breakfast.

Inside we're still fluid – nothing's solidified
except our resolve not to move.
The boundaries between us indistinct.
Heat overflows, drowsy as opium.

A familiar, ancient smell
damps down civilised thought –
to be up and doing.
The air, moist and receptive,
wants to stick to our skin.

We're feeling magnanimous so give in
and kick off the blanket,
listening to the morning
get on with its business
while we get on with ours.

# Part 2

# The Mother Workshops

**Exercise 1:  Similes**

The Mother


The mother's skin feels sheer as a moth's wing.

The mother's eyes look pale
as winter sky nearly empty of rain.

The mother's nose sniffs
like a dog in unfamiliar territory.

The mother's hip explodes like peanut brittle.
She prods the world with a cane,
peevish for answers.

The mother loses nouns and verbs,
flaps like a bird counting chicks in her nest,
keeps coming up with the wrong number.

The mother is a still pool,
waiting for me to ripple with my words.

I stir and stir.

## Exercise 2: Exposition

### What it Means
*after 80 years*

What do you think of
when you can't think?
What memories taunt
when you can't remember?

You recognise each physical ache
in that well-thumbed body.
Nerves almost welcome the pulse
like phone calls from friends.

Dependable pain swells the air.
You hear the thunder,
know what comes after.

But the past is a shooting star.
Is that an afterglow out in space
or did that planetary mist
always cloud the dome?

Better to stay home where the mind's propped up.
A photo, a lamp, a glass figurine –
flint against which you can light.
For minutes, the truth of a life gleams.

Relaxing as a holiday, this physical world.
You remember you should know
what it means.

## Exercise 3:  Syntax

### Verbal Salad at the Mall

### 1.  The Food Hall

She offers her salad to everyone,
mixing the crisp parts of speech.
"Now it's getting car, car.
I smell through my girls," she smiles.

Addicted to toddlers in primary colours
(*first words, last words* are the same),
she gawks and coos at bemused mothers.
"I was there once upon a time," she explains.

As we stroll arm in arm, her face turns
like a sunflower to a new source –
a world in the process of losing its names.
Soon every day is the first.

In the beginning was the word
and so all dissolves in the chaos of forms.
A paradise of a merry-go-round,
the mall's centrepiece:
horses' tails, children's screams, lions' manes –
a swirling feast.

### 2.  The Fountain

From the atrium the fountain calls.
We wander over to hear
water pop like corn on sea horses' backs,
dolphins diving nowhere.
Her eyes reflect the iridescent tiles,
the things she cannot ask.

Questions and answers are enemies.
It's time to go, but I refuse to say so.

She is happy in this moment,
leaning on another body,
feeling the wet whisper,
watching unruly flakes of light
somersault and melt into themselves
as the sun jolts overhead.

Consistent and eternal at our backs –
this place of miracles – as we leave.
She doesn't see, late at night,
when the power shudders off,
how the pool smooths
like a face in its final sleep.

## Exercise 4:  Synecdoche

Legs

The part I notice most is the legs. Muscleless, withered, muscular or anaemic – they are old. I notice the veins especially. Veins don't really look like ropes beneath the skin; they are like tube worms. Or Alice in Wonderland pathways, seen from the air. They run thick and dark for a time, then disappear underground to resurface a few kilometres on. They arch and angle, thin and refine themselves. They mark out odd parcels of territory – under whose control?

Look at the dimpled thighs, the swishing flesh of the dancers at Senior Citizens' Centres. The silhouettes of the women – some all bust, no waist, some no bust or waist, just a torso glued to spindly legs, stencilled with blue.

Is that why they dye their hair such outrageous colours – volcano red is popular, or copper – to lift the eyes up from below, to blind us? Then we won't remember those insidious pathways that slink underground. And wonder, where do they go?

# Exercise 5: Memoir

## Metaphorical Life Studies

"Or it's a story
(Because stories are safe, because stories are sound, because
stories make the world go round.)"
Morris Lurie, *Whole Life*

Is there something that I remember most? Her voice and the way she moved across a room. She was always humming a tune or singing along with the radio. She had a rich alto voice. Any minute she might burst into a full-fledged performance. If we had lived in movieland, there would have been an orchestra hidden in the broom cupboard, and my mother could have danced out of the kitchen with a chorus of tuxedoed men at her back and carried off a grand production number, 1930s style.

She was instinctively graceful, a born dancer. In the 1950s she managed to cajole my father into taking ballroom dancing lessons, so at least he could lead her around competently at the rare functions they went to – the Builders' Federation Annual Dinners, family weddings or bar mitzvahs. Her soul was in her legs and voice – that's the only time she looked truly happy. No reservations in front of an audience. No demands on either side. All they had to do was watch and all she had to do was be watched.

The family story was that she had left school in eleventh grade so she could make money to help her family. She had desperately wanted to be a dancer, but her poor Russian immigrant parents couldn't afford tap lessons. Ironically, her best friend in school was forced to take them. Good fortune for my mother. She picked the girl's brain and made her teach each week's new steps, practising on her own. "But once you know a time step," my mother said, "you're home free." And that was all she had to perform at her first audition. One day she left her office job at the Folly Frock House and headed for midtown Manhattan. When she returned home to the Bronx, she had a new career.

Marian Hollis is top row, far right.

At sixteen she was making more money as a dancer than her father, Benjamin, a carpenter who had suffered a horrendous accident, losing a foot and some fingers in the 1920s. There was no workers' compensation then, so the City of New York gave him a newstand to run near City Hall. That's how he supported his family. For years my mother sent money home to help my grandmother. She was always proud of doing that – the good daughter, the working daughter, but not the favourite like her sister Bertha, who stayed at home until she married. My mother always said that she was an enigma to her parents. But how could orthodox Russian Jewish immigrants figure out a showgirl in the family?

I remember holidaying at resort hotels in the Catskill Mountains in upstate New York in the 1950s – the Nevele and the Concord. Was I eight, nine, ten? At afternoon dances I loved to cha cha, waltz or mambo with my mother (who had taught me), because I knew people were watching. We had fun showing off.

The social directors held dancing contests, and the instructors partnered the entrants. My mother won not only bottles of champagne, but free weekends for doing the peabody – a swirling, complicated dance that took up the entire stage. In that breathless flow my mother would tilt her head back, leaning into each spin. Once you saw her perform you knew that she had to win. She made the instructor look good with her practised stage presence. Every movement said "professional."

Years later my mother told me that she had worked in shows at these hotels in the summers. That's when I found out that the name "Nevele" was a reversal of eleven – for the family's eleven children. And that she had been in love with a boy called "Jucky" in the Catskills, whose real name she couldn't recall. After her death I found a photo of him, too: Jucky, another boy in the band.

Professionals aren't necessarily stars or rich. They only inspire awe in amateurs, relatives or lovers. In the show biz world, they commanded respect. My mother was never out of work because she was competent, punctual, versatile and, for many years, a flaming redhead. She became a Chester Hale Girl, kicked high

Marian Hollis is far right, sitting on the car.

in choruses at the Brooklyn Paramount Theatre, the Apollo in Harlem, the Capitol. She was a soubrette, singing and dancing solo, she toured the country, she tapdanced across the boards of Radio City Music Hall. Her crowning achievement was to be a mistress of ceremonies in the Panama Canal Zone, for two years introducing acts in a night club and also hosting a radio program for servicemen. As a girl watching the Rockettes at Radio City, I felt an arrogant thrill knowing that my mother, sitting beside me, had once been up there under the coloured lights.

And the proof of her glory days? All the photos. Another world in pictures my father had meticulously hung on specially made aluminium racks in our basement in suburban Queens. Two entire walls commemorating my mother's show business life. Skimpy costumes shimmered, slick as icicles or diaphanous as cobwebs. My mother always looked glamorous, even in the zany hats they wore. I remember the tap dancing shoes with chunky curved heels and wide bows. There were pictures with the leading names of the day: Milton Berle, Ben Blue, the Ritz Brothers and Jimmy Durante, one with Alice Faye before she was famous. Marian Hollis was my mother's stage name, "Hollis" picked off a billboard when she realised that Mary Cohen couldn't be a star's name. And why didn't she make it? Was she not talented enough, beautiful enough, persistent enough? Was it the musicians she kept falling for?

Another story. When my mother told my grandmother that she was engaged to my father, she simply said, "Fine. I'll believe it when I see it." This was the fifth engagement. But my father wasn't a musician, like the saxophone player, on tour in California, to whom my mother was promised at the time. He was a carpenter, a builder – solid, dependable, focused – an ambitious man determined not to be poor, although he had only finished tenth grade in school and had nothing. Another child of Russian immigrants. Marian Hollis was doing well, but for a woman nearing thirty, well wasn't enough. Jerry Kroll was the future. He wouldn't drift off in the night like a bittersweet refrain.

They met on a blind date – her first and probably his, since he was a handsome Brooklyn playboy. It was the kind of date that begins as a disaster and gets worse. She travelled from her parents' home in the Bronx to do a friend a favour – "Please, Marian, this boy I like is staying with Jerry, he wants to pay him back and I've been talking about you so much."

Marian was meeting them at the Astor Hotel in Manhattan. Of course the car had a blow-out and they were incredibly late. When they arrived she was surly, she was nasty, but Jerry was dazzled by her confidence. And she became intrigued by his passion to get somewhere, to make himself over. When introduced to the new boyfriend, my grandmother rehearsed her stock line:

"Nu? So when is the marriage taking place *this* time?"

And my mother always replied, "I'm not sure, Mom, I'll let you know when."

But within a few months he had formally proposed to his all-American glamour girl, his songbird. She would learn to be his wife.

And she did. And in a way she never forgave him or her daughters for being part of the conspiracy. Like many vibrant, intelligent women before her, she became frustrated by domesticity. She got what she wanted – security – and then paid for it, and made us pay, becoming the all-American bitch-mother, whom, only years later, I would understand.

When my sister and I were older she became a volunteer worker, first at Creedmore State Mental Hospital and then at the Institute for the Crippled and Disabled. She taught patients how to tile table tops, learned photo oil colouring so she could teach it. She was praised and thanked, she won awards. My father would say, "What do you need to do that for? It might be dangerous with those people. They're crazy." Or – "Why do you need to knock yourself out? You have enough to do." Running a house and family. Running us. Running to keep herself busy, tiring herself out, going crazy.

After my mother's death, my sister and I came across two small statues – gold plastic, with little labels pasted on the front. She had only won them a few years earlier. I took the statue that said

Senior Citizen
1st Place
Charleston.

It weighed so little and the sticky tape holding the label was peeling off. At the end, she weighed less than a healthy ten-year-old, less than I probably did when I used to dance with her. Her bones were hollow, but they still longed to dance. After breaking both hips, she was stiff and awkward. Yet music would still transform her, as if someone with a remote control in another room demanded that she rise and sway.

And on those days when she felt too weak or dizzy to stand, she would hand dance to Frank Sinatra, Tony Bennett or Perry Como, whatever old record we could find, even the newcomer, Barbara Streisand – her swollen fingers making graceful patterns in front of her face, keeping perfect time with the music. She would sit for an hour, never tiring, her hands using the air as a stage. She was dancing, she was living.

# Exercise 6: Writing to Music

The Showgirl in the Wandering Garden
Alzheimer's Unit
Florida

1

My mother was a natural dancer born
to perform. Her body never forgot
the rhythms or the gestures of a song.
A girl, she had willingly made this pledge –

to be a star, forsaking all for the stage.
Although she barely made it out of the chorus,
the lyrics of "Moonlight Bay," "Begin the Beguine,"
outlasted memory of her husband's name.

In a flash of her skirts, it seemed, he was gone.
The band took a break and suddenly, she was old.
Yet whenever the diamond needle hit the groove
she jumped to meet a stranger in the night.

2

She crumples now when the music stops,
her face slowly drains of every chord.
Awkwardly she rises with the group
to promenade in The Wandering Garden.

She hums a bar or two and nods and hums.
The paths repeat themselves just like the old
who know somehow that they will shuffle out
when light begins to flicker. In the dusk

her body finally learns another tune
as fragile and as slow as healing bones –
composed for her alone but incomplete
until she can perfect that final step.

# Exercise 7:  Making Use of Errors

RIP Errata

JULIUS ROBERT KROLL
BELOVED HUSBAND
AND FATHER
OCTOBER 13, 1911
SEPTEMBER 24, 1979

My father is buried in a decaying section of Brooklyn where we are afraid to go, relaxing in Section Comp K, Plot 310, two berths' wide, a legacy of the bargain-basement mentality – two for the price of one, irresistible to a businessman. He is waiting for one-third of my mother's ashes. (My sister and I have a third each.) Once that fraction is buried, we will never visit again.

Note the date: 1979. My mother has just turned sixty-eight on September 13th. When my parents had first met, she had told my father that she was born the same year as he was – 1912.  But she had never seen a birth certificate. In the 1950s, however, she finally needed one for a passport because my father wanted to take her to Europe. After months hassling with the Department of Health, it produced a copy that reported that she was one year older than her husband. My father went around complaining, "I've married an older woman." A clever older woman.

My mother has been shattered by my father's unforeseen abandonment; she is not thinking clearly. I have to organise documents, schedules, phone numbers for her in the next three weeks before I return to Australia, but she is competent to manage afterwards.

The tumour (a lipoma) that will begin to cause blackouts in a year snuggles in her brain, comfortable as a foetus growing at an infinitesimal pace.  It is not malicious, remains her companion for nearly twenty years, causing minor disturbance. And the doctors have always said that it does not affect memory, although the Dilantin she will soon begin taking can.

Is what happened next a kind of vaudeville joke on my parents, a dress rehearsal of how her mind will perform in future?

*My mother orders my father's headstone. He was born on Columbus Day, October 12, 1912.  At least she gets the month right, but she has given him her birth day and year.*

## Exercise 8: Found Poem

### Checkup at the Memory Disorder Unit

"How have you been feeling?"

"Fine."
>    The old woman knows enough to smile.

>    The doctor knows enough to note these facts –
>    the "fine" and "smile."

"How has she been feeling?"
>    he asks her aide.

"Fine."
>    The aide is twenty-six
>    and knows enough to smile
>    to keep her job.

"What's this?"
>    he asks his patient,
>    pointing to his watch.

>    Her face drains, then turns sly.
"If *you* don't know,
I'm not going to tell you."

>    She knows enough to smile.

## Exercise 9: Villanelle

### Portrait of a Lady

I try to salvage what she was, and yet
exhausted words are what I can recall.
"Don't worry," she says at last, "I don't forget."

I pack her life up, seal it with regret.
Memories of photos stain the wall.
I try to salvage what she was, and yet

doctors and lawyers know the etiquette.
They control her life now, after all.
"Don't worry," she says at last, "I don't forget."

She still sings and dances as a coquette
although she now seems pitifully small.
I try to salvage what she was, and yet

she holds a toothbrush like a cigarette.
She's never been the same since that last fall.
"Don't worry," she says at last, "I don't forget."

Was she ever that passionate brunette
draped in photos with an ermine shawl?
I try to salvage what she was, and yet –
"Don't worry," she says at last, "and don't forget."

# Exercise 10:  A Postmortem Workshop

"Ennui"
**Poem by Marian Kroll, circa 1980**

(written for "Don't Be Afraid to Write!"
C. W. Post Office of Continuing Education course)


## Ennui

The postman's ring brings me to my feet
My daughter's letter comes, like a long awaited treat
Her news is good, all is well says she,
"But why don't you write more often to me?"
So, write I will, but what about?
The varied moods, that put me in doubt,
of the pointless chatter I engage in
On the phone? No one to relate to, after the day's chores are done?
The infrequent comfort I find, ministering to those less fortunate
Who think me so kind is balm to my ego, and at times brings me some peace
of mind. The arts and crafts, they've had their fling
Gaily hooked rugs lie on the floor
Pictures decorate the walls
Plants are abloom, the house neat and clean

All mute testimony to an ongoing dream.
But Ennui returns, in spite of a new dress
Gold chains jangle round my neck, evidence of an indulgent husband
who knows nothing of my distress.
But, not enough, not enough, cries a melancholy voice,
What is there within me, I am seeking to express?
What does all this mean?
Will Life with it's promise of spring bud anew?
Leave all frailties behind, give me renewed strength in body and mind?
Stop grasping at straws, as I've done in the past
Perhaps this time I'll hold on more firmly
To find my Destiny at last.

# A Postmortem Workshop

I'm reading this poem with two minds engaged – the daughter, the writing teacher. Even retyping "Ennui" I'm inclined to fiddle, can't resist changing the number 1 to an I, but leave the apostrophe in it's. I somehow like the capital E in DEstiny. The right hand reaches out instinctively for the metaphorical red pen. The left hand is indecisive.

Should I punish myself with clichés and use that hand to clutch my heart? She is dead. I cannot stretch out to comfort her. I always knew that she understood herself, but this clearly? Yes, sometimes. I suppose that's one of the reasons I could keep loving her despite her mind games – at a safe distance, where only the voice on the phone was to be feared. My father had bullied her all their married life – she called him her "sparring partner," but she took most of the verbal blows. So she developed her own subtler style of assault: the fractious mutter, and worse, the threatening silence. Her unsaid words could always scorch: ungrateful, unworthy, unkind child.

More than a decade later words became the enemy, the means of her betrayal, but in 1980 she thought she had found another use for them besides defense. Maybe they would tell her about herself. So how well did she perform in "Ennui"?

I can still be objective here, note the clichés and punctuation errors as well as the facility with words, the frustrated energy. She admitted with a deprecating laugh that her writing teacher insisted that she had potential:

> *Give me six months and I can whip this poet*
> *into shape. Offer contemporary models, suggest subtler*
> *strategies, train her ear. My seventy-year-old model*
> *student – see what I've accomplished with her?*

Then I put on my reading glasses and get up close and personal with this piece of paper. I notice "the indulgent husband" who died in 1979, although the significance of the new dress, the gold chains still makes sense. He has left her well-provided for; she need never worry – but she does. He has told her nothing about his finances through their marriage, not prepared her for any responsibility.

After all, like any good Jewish husband, he thought he would live as long as a Biblical patriarch, to cherish and protect so his wife need never bother her pretty little head. The handsome businessman/builder, with silver-flecked hair and moustache, intended to supervise the flourishing of his family, to watch what he had begat beget in their turn. It's ironic that he never lived to see any of his grandchildren. Why? He worked seven days a week to provide against bleaker times. The Depression might have ended in 1939, but the idea of it wore his heart out as easily as a bargain-basement pump. Except for the watching and enjoying part, my father fulfilled, more or less, his life plan, despite the swindlings and disappointments doled out by former friends.

And this poem is part of my mother's comment on success. Ennui. She shopped, dressed well, volunteered, wrote the odd letter, composed occasional poems, cleaned and polished and swept, hooked rugs, tiled tables, coloured photographs, did needlepoint, knitted, crocheted. I have samples of her indefatigable energy everywhere as the poem details.

As a good writing teacher, a dutiful daughter, I note how the list rattles on until it comes to the end of the line. Where to now, poem? Please, not a cop out. Go somewhere. But no, it peters out with vague questions. And where as a writing teacher, as a daughter, could I have told her to go?

I can speculate on the shape of the "ongoing dream" at my parents' wedding. After the war, they went on to live it with the rest of 1950s America. But this was my mother's dream, alone. Or was she only in love with the idea of dreaming? She saw my sister and I set goals and plug away over the years. She was proud and jealous of our dreaming, our realising. We had at least moved from point A to point B. But enough of us. Back to the mother's poem. She needs the limelight she gave up at her wedding, the centre stage she missed.

The heart I spoke of earlier, which I could have clutched with my left hand, murmurs and falters now with the rhythm of the last lines. Where to, poem? Its list of distractions could march off into the mist, till exhaustion got the better of writer, reader, woman.

"To leave frailty behind." Yet "frail" was not a word that ever sprang to mind about my mother, at least until her final years. "Stop grasping at straws?" Of course, that's what any therapist would say. Consider your options. Find a DEstiny. Commit yourself. Agreed. But these are the words that pulse with a migraine's insistence beneath the surface of the poem: to what, to what, to what?

## Exercise 11:  Sonnet

## The Toxic Parent

See the skull and crossbones under the skin?
Beneath the high cheekbones, the Roman nose,
the disapproving mouth, the withered chin –
the aging parent's face – the venom flows.
They loved us once, but now they've turned within.
Skewed memories, the kind that decompose
and recompose, forgetting their origins,
return dressed in the prodigal's clothes
to disinherit us. Study the discipline
of being always in the wrong.  Pose
as counsellors, caretakers, chauffeurs, children –
nothing will work. We're there for them to oppose.
Steep yourselves in their lives, let them be free
until old age grants you immunity.

## Exercise 12:  The subject is . . .

### Smiles of a Summer's Afternoon
### Unknown Woman at the Alzheimer's Unit

Impassive, she watches the others
as the old-time tunes switch on.

Immaculate old men in pressed white shirts,
women with skin mottled like camouflage
are jolted to their feet,
which remember fox trot and waltz.

Her face is insulated.
The dancers could be copulating or
beating each other to death
instead of risking their hips –
a fall, thrill of the day.

Then Mona Lisa's smile appears,
some vessel of memory splits.
She worries her mouth, searching for lost tastes –

an almost rotten peach at summer's end,
a dog biscuit snitched from a bowl,
ignorant lips, tingling in the dusk.

The smile lasts like ices
on a blistering afternoon.
Tongue remembers that sticky sweetness
evaporating in the dark.

## Exercise 13: Paternal Interlude

Kroll Roofing Inc
New York City
1954

My father's workshop was a man's place.
I knew because of all the men who worked there.
The only woman – Edith the bookkeeper –
stayed clean in her dingy office.
A blowsy mountain in a flowery dress,
she told me to sit and wait and then forgot.

My father was never on time.
There was always another call to make,
an employee to be pulled into line.
The calculator's hiccups, the typewriter's clack
were polite compared to the squeal of machines
outside the door where the real world began.

I suffered from cosmic boredom,
would fidget with magazines,
count the ashtray's butts,
then finally sneak to the shop
vast as a gymnasium.

I wandered past sheet-metal stacked
like walls of frozen water,
found coins of tin and copper.
I heard words I was not supposed to use
hit the faraway rafters.

Then one day there they were –
the other women lost in this man's world.
Redheads, blondes, brunettes
pinned up in a cubbyhole,
their nipples pointing at me.

They knew I wasn't supposed to see them naked.
I somehow knew, too.
When the foreman walked by
I read out the names of the companies they worked for.
None of them looked like Edith.

They bent their legs at odd angles,
licked or pursed their lips.
Their skin was sweaty with axle grease
and plum sauce from takeout Chinese.

One of the men couldn't wait for summer.
A month had been ripped off a calendar
like a pair of lace panties
for there was Miss July in a straw hat,
a pair of high-heeled sandals,
and it was still only May.

After that first day, whenever I could,
I would sneak out to visit the girls.
We had our own club
and new members every month.

Did I want to be like them when I grew up?
Did I love them for their raspberry lips
and skin as smooth as coconut ice?
What secrets did we share,
an island of women surrounded by dangers
I could not yet name?

## Exercise 14:  Wordplay

### The Incredible Lightness of Forgetting

for my sister

" . . . your mother's mental status remains unchanged. She still has receptive aphasia."


*New Mail.*  It's you again – with attachments.
I can't bear to read some days
the doctors' linear columns,

their self-absorbed drone,
their balancing act with statistics.
Her baffled face wobbles between the lines.

If only I were clever enough to forget
the disease they never mentioned
to our mother.

But she knew. For a while.
For a while, I don't want to know
the letter that begins the alphabet.

The incredible lightness of being
a featherweight mind!
I'd strip away all wit,

relax into dementia like a bath,
listen to bubbles whisper
lavender-scented nothings in my ears.

No luck. I'm memory-obsessed.
"I know that face."
"What was that actor's name

that flashed across the screen?"
Twenty years ago I would have guessed
as fast as you could strike a match.

Still, I have my rituals to cope.
I rake the alphabet like crumbling leaves,
sifting for clues.

Tonight, rust haloes the moon.
Grass aches with frost.
I open the file, print the doctors' words.

The fire talks in feverish tongues,
then settles down to business,
becoming a heap of ashen bones.

The ghost of our mother's mind
floats across these pages,
blurring the print.

## Exercise 15: Factions

### Strange Interludes

This story was told to me by another traveller, just passing
through. It took place in a foreign country, as everything does.
Margaret Atwood, "Circe / Mud Poems"

*Friar Barnardine:* Thou hast committed–
*Barabas:* Fornication: but that was in another country;
And besides the wench is dead.
Christopher Marlowe, *The Jew of Malta*

I would like to say that this story was told to me by someone I
met in a pub or at work and that it takes place in a foreign country.
But it doesn't. We want to deny it, but stories all take place here.

i

Once there was a woman who, like many before her, chronicled
her baby's milestones: first cries, tears, gestures. And then the
miraculous first words: "Mama, dada, more." Whatever.

Her son, like others before him, said things that granted
his parents the gift of cathartic laughter. He quantified his
immeasurable feelings: "I love you 100 kilometres of distance."
And then he perplexed them with philosophy pared down to a
fingernail's width. When he asked, "What does God look like?",
and the adults could not agree on a particular shape, he announced,
"God is square."

He was as clever as most toddlers, a trial and an arch-seducer.
But the child grew and became a monosyllabic adolescent. Enough
said.

ii

His grandmother, however, had grown as well. For years her
conversation had been loaded with innuendo, laced with guilt.
Accordingly, not much had passed between mother and daughter.

But in her eighty-second year, as if she had been spending weekends at a Californian encounter group that told her to "Be Here Now," the grandmother gradually became another woman.

Suddenly the daughter was taking notes again. Disintegration became charming and achingly comic, the same weird mix of the toddler's diction.

"I don't want to hold you too much, because my marbles might roll . . . ," she says to one daughter.

"Your cliche was *so* beautiful," she says to another.

Even the TV sends messages, although like the oracle at Delphi's riddles, they might be indecipherable. She watches Robin "Errol Flynn" Hood racing through Sherwood Forest, outstripping his Merry Men, looking for his own true maid. "Marian, Marian," he calls.

"What? Why is he calling me?" the grandmother asks her companion, pointing at the TV. "How does he know my name?"

"Names are the essential," says Samuel Beckett. At least she still knows her own.

iii

This story *was* told to me by someone in another country and yes, the woman in question is dead.

Once a nurse went to a wildlife park and took photos of all the happy animals. They were happy, the tourists were assured, to be protected. Happy to be alive on this up-to-date ark, chosen species together, marooned in suburban Florida.

She snapped pictures of elephants, ostriches, camels, hippopotami, lions and zebras. She was dazzled by the exotic display. This would be stimulating, too, she thought, for her elderly employer, whose vocabulary had been reduced, like a French sauce, to the rich essentials.

One afternoon she sat down with her patient near a window. Together, they sifted through the pictures. The widow held up each in turn, pondering. The elephant. The ostrich. The camel. The hippopotamus wallowing in mud sluggish as chocolate syrup. She spent longer on that one (loving chocolate as she did). Finally, the zebra whose stripes went in several directions like the woman's syntax.

The nurse smiled expectantly. Her patient looked suspicious. She flicked through the photos once more, refusing to glance up, then lifted her face with a knowing smile. "They're not Americans," she said.

## Exercise 16:  Poetry as Catharsis

### Lift  Off

Like sugar cubes, language crumbles
and you grow sweeter.
Does forgetting how to curse
cancel desire?

Confusion short-circuits anger,
helps us to fuse.
I move beyond understanding,
become generic daughter,
nameless and finally loved.

Amazing – tension dissolves
that had smothered us like an oil slick.
What survived and suffered below?

Enough.

I see you above,
knowing it's almost lift off,
balanced on a wire in all weathers,

singing non sequiturs,
unconscious of the power
shooting through underneath.

## Exercise 17: Generational Comparisons

## Now You See Me, Now You Don't

Children love to hide – behind hands, behind furniture, behind the dependable bulk of their parents. "Now you see me, now you don't" is a refrain weaving through childhood. Hide and seek is a more sophisticated version of this kind of bodily control. The child decides when and how he is seen. She knows if she giggles, she gives herself away. If he wants, he can use magic to withhold himself. My son once spent an hour being invisible. He threw a magic saddle blanket over himself and, presto, no one could bother him.

What elderly person wants to be invisible? The wish to disappear, to slip beneath the gaze of others, only occurs when they feel shame. If they are dizzy, if they can't control their mouths, if they have soiled themselves, they do not want anyone to notice.

My mother knew two years before she died that she was fading into the background, that no adult wanted to notice her any more. I realised this one morning when we were having breakfast alone. Her partner, Al, had gone away for a week to visit his daughter in another state and he had made sure – after countless international phone calls – that he had booked his trip during my annual visit.

We were sitting at the round kitchen table. Occasionally my mother would lift a piece of bagel to her mouth. Sometimes she would put it in and chew tentatively; sometimes she would forget why she had picked it up in the first place. Then she would drop it with annoyance and push the plate away, saying, "That's enough. Enough." Or "Too much. I can't eat any more."

I had managed to coax her into swallowing the five pills that she was presently taking. Every morning the same ritual: explain what the pills were for; hold them out one by one; make sure they were swallowed; praise her efforts. Once I had to call the doctor to have him verify that, yes, he had said she needed them all.

But we had jumped that hurdle by 8:30. Now we sat in silence. Her hand hovered over the bagel crumbs. I sipped my tea and marvelled, yet again, how patient I had become. I could probably sit for at least another ten minutes without becoming nervous.

After eight minutes I gave in. I had to move so I stood, and immediately had to sit down because my mother tottered up as well. "No, stay there, Mom, I just want to get something." I settled her before sprinting to the living room. I grabbed a large photo in a plastic holder and brought it back.

"Remember them?" I displayed her grandsons, aged two and five, sitting in her New York apartment in 1986, naked on her bed in front of the TV. The backdrop, her blue and silver wallpaper, a bit like gift wrapping. The boys were the gifts. They could be the morning's topic of conversation. Again.

We spoke about them, or I did, reminding her of this or that thing they had said or done. Then we lapsed into silence. All at once, she took my hand. "They don't want to talk to me any more," she said in a low but clear voice. I looked into her eyes, marble blue with tawny flecks. She knew exactly what she was saying.

But I wasn't sure. "Who?" I squeezed her hand.

"I know. They don't want to talk to me, just to him."

She meant her partner. "I'm sure that's not true, Mom." That was the appropriate soothing phrase.

"They speak to him, but they don't look at me any more. They don't talk to me."

I couldn't say she was wrong, I could only squeeze her fingers. She didn't know much these days, so how could I deny her the little truths she could still grasp?

I remembered walking around their self-contained village in the late afternoons over the years. We would run into their friends for a ritual exchange of news, but they had been noticing my mother's deterioration recently. She said inappropriate things, or stopped the conversation while she searched for a word that had slipped out of reach like a coin through a grate. All she could hear was its echo below.

Now they had instituted another routine. They would be loud and cuddly, hugging or kissing my mother, but within a minute, they would be talking only to Al. They would forget even to look at her. She simply faded into the dusk. Sometimes she would become angry and sulk on the walk home, or make him pay by her caustic mood when they reached their apartment. More often her face became vacant, as she simply accepted what their behaviour implied– soon no one would be home.

Our eyes. The same colour, the same slick surface. She knew I understood, and smiled with relief. Finally, someone was listening to her again, someone was looking at her, but not to judge. She didn't have to perform.

For the next half hour she talked in more or less coherent sentences, telling me her fears – of losing her mind, of abandonment: "He wants to put me away. I'll have to go soon." Telling me of her love for my sister and me.

Then she stood up with such purpose that I let her hobble off alone. She was steadier on her feet, words rebalancing the world. She came back and pressed something into my hand – two one hundred dollar bills. "I want you to have this," she said. I had no idea where she had found them, but Al had mentioned several months ago that he thought she had been hiding money around the apartment.

She had found, not only the bills, smelling of stale perfume, but a trace of her past – the self-sufficient dancer helping her family, the mother giving a gift to her daughter.

She made more sense to me in that half hour than she had in the past twenty years. She trusted me completely and she wasn't afraid to do it. Neither of us had anything to lose. Even language had declared a truce.

# Exercise 18: Re-Vision

"Re-vision – the act of looking back, of seeing with fresh eyes,
of entering an old text from a new critical direction, is for us more than a
chapter in cultural history: it is an act of survival. Until we can understand
the assumptions in which we are drenched we cannot know ourselves."

Adrienne Rich, "When We Dead Awaken: Writing as Re-Vision" (1971)


## Human Remains


A depressing way to spend an afternoon,
knowing yourself.

Some drink, do drugs, screw themselves silly.
Others with less guts or more sense
read thrillers or romance,
watch videos, sip coffee,
work themselves into a trance

all to avoid having that face
take shape in the internal pool.
The name of the game
is sully the waters.
Is the above true?

Here, take this test.
Choose one below. Make up the rest.

a) Whose portrait have I drawn?

b) Can exercises train the truth?

c) Who's fit enough to know?

d) How you do address a dead woman,
who ends up in a cardboard box,
labelled *Human Remains?*

The crux of the problem, mother –
I've lost the chance to revise
how we were.
I can only recall what was –
repeat, reshuffle, lament –
which word is better?

What I think I knew
about me,
about you.

Is this an act of survival,
using you as a text?

Is this an act of betrayal,
displaying your weakness and bitterness?

Is this an act of love,
or of searching for it?

This is my way of making you survive,
asking the unanswerable questions.

## Exercise 19: Meditations on Food


## The Philosophy of Chocolate


### i  Feasting on Memories


My mother gave up being an adventurous showgirl by 1941, when she married, but she incorporated her passionate and unorthodox soul into her cooking. She took the standard elementary school line that the United States was a melting pot of nationalities literally.

Psychologists say that smell is one of the most enduring senses, and my nose twitches that it's true. Her specialties waft around me still. I can never forget her pickled shrimp, steeped in a marinade of red and black peppercorns, cloves, sliced onions, exotic vinegars and oils. Her lasagna was overweighted with three kinds of cheese – mozzarella, farmer's and pot – which made it fork-provokingly sticky.

Once in a gourmet fit my mother cooked Canard Montmorency for my college boyfriend. I remember the aroma of the duck giving up its fat in the oven, its skin shrinking on its frame to become a crisp tawny suit. Then the sweet-tart cherry sauce, lumpy as if it concealed the hearts of tiny fairytale creatures, simmering on the stove.

At every meal we had salads doused in her homemade dressing, which was laced with deep brown anchovy paste that made you grimace, crumbly parmesan cheese that looked like old plaster and red wine vinegar that never forgot its alcohol origins.

My mother orchestrated some stupendous Thanksgiving meals. She would rise early to place the turkey in the oven and then religiously baste its hide with a mixture of oil, butter and spices to keep it moist and tan as the skin of a star on Malibu Beach. Brewing within, flavouring the body subtly over the hours, was the herb stuffing, some years laced with roasted chestnuts, crunchy breadcrumbs, pine nuts. And when the turkey was served on the oversized white china platter, it had true stage presence.

This was what my mother bequeathed to my sister and me – a love of food and its presentation. No doubt, part of the reason she lost her passion was that we grew up, moved out, my father died and who was there left to cook for?

Then, in her last years, she forgot how. She couldn't remember the familiar sequences laid out in cookbooks for bachelors, students and new homemakers. But the most unkind cut of all in this embarrassing disease, which made it difficult to feed herself, was that she lost the ability to enjoy. Her taste buds weakened, she had trouble chewing. Her mouth couldn't decide how to attack what was dropped inside. To squash, to chomp, simply to swallow? Exhausting.

*ii La Dolce Vita*

But finally, there were tender mercies. I discovered the transcendence of chocolate. I could bring it as a gift and know it would be greeted with a moist mouth. I could watch my mother puzzle over which mottled Belgian seashell to select before she let one dissolve, happy to be living only in that sweet moment.

Here is the philosophy of chocolate: in all its forms, chocolate marks the stages of a life. First, it is a reward or bribe given by parents. Then it's an instant high for a volatile teen. Next a token of lust from a lover. After childbirth and unwanted pounds, it becomes a sin, a forbidden treat secreted in a drawer underneath too-tight lingerie. Even dieters enjoy low-fat shadows, as sweet self-control melts on the tongue.

Finally chocolate is all we have. Our lives slim down to basics, the first principles of pleasure: tactile and oral.

### iii My Mother's Last Suppers

This visit I bring edible works of art,
a gallery in a box, fine as a pearl brooch –
the flaws part of their allure.
And they contain tender mercies:
glacé cherries, liqueurs and mocha creams,
marzipan, caramel and nougat.

She selects an oval piece,
its curves smooth as an African Queen's,
coloured jarrah that fades into black,
bittersweet as life itself.

A button of creamy white perches on the top,
inviting teeth to snip.
Then there's an etched border,
decorative as a cornice.

I have no idea what's inside.
That is the challenge that awaits my mother.
She bites off half . At once her eyes flicker
as her tongue begins this last great adventure.

# Exercise 20: Personification:  My Mother's Pathology

## Making Peace

Let's call this woman Anne.
She likes her clients on a first-name basis –
that's all they can remember.

She dresses well in skirt and blouse –
raw silk and natural wool.
My mother feels at ease.

Some good has come of knowing her.
She sits between us, has these last few years,
helping us make peace.

Nights we play with scrabbled words
while heart-throbs croon away the hours.
I shuffle photos like a pack of cards,
where every one's an ace.

Therapy's almost done.
Anne sweeps the air with her palm
as if to clear a space.

Suddenly, the ceiling opens up.
Clouds surge across the sky
like bloated corpses.

"No," she says, "don't be morbid."
All right. Full as babies after a meal.

I hold my mother's hand.
We watch shapes ebb and flow.
What will they be,
these creatures of combined imagination,
backlit by the failing sun?

We've no one left to please except ourselves.

– A goddess of the screen with ash-blonde hair?

– A unicorn with a coat so sheer
its blue veins shimmer through?

– Two women made of sea foam,
clinging together,
as the evening tide washes them away,
one after the other.

## Exercise 21: Using Letters

RIP Mark Twain –
who said once that reports of his death were greatly exaggerated.

Every letter from one year, 1987, written on aerogrammes that have a bright colour inset of Mark Twain and this quotation:

> "I came in with Halley's Comet in 1835. It is coming again next year, and I expect to go out with it. It will be the greatest disappointment of my life if I don't go out with Halley's Comet."

Now there was a man who knew his own mind, how he wanted to be remembered. A grand exit for someone with a sense of symmetry. How many of us think about planning our exit, our testimonials?

If my mother had been capable, would she have wanted to compose her own epitaph?

> Here lies a former showgirl, a voracious reader, a community reporter, a dedicated volunteer, an erstwhile writer of occasional verse . . .

"Beloved Mother of" hardly seems enough.

By the time my mother died in 1998, all her brothers and sisters, and most of her brothers-in-law and sisters-in-law, were dead. A few nodding acquaintances in Florida were left. My sister and I stood in the funeral home's back room, painted a washed-out green like an old cafeteria kitchen. In neat blue and grey suits, the gay funeral director and his assistant stood with hands by their sides. We were waiting for them to leave, but we didn't have the presence of mind to ask. They had no ritual prepared for this; they weren't used to our request, since apparently no one wanted to stay for the cremation. Looking around the room, I could understand why.

The doors of the crematorium opened. The heat pulsed out but it wasn't threatening. The flames were as expected – carmine, saffron, vermilion. Check the Thesaurus. We watched her slide into them, being watched ourselves by these men.

I remember the sound of the flames more than their colour. It was as if she were being rolled onto a freeway, the traffic swishing around and past. She was being dissolved by noise, not heat. Her forehead was already slick, the skin browning off. In anticipation of this? In a few minutes, she had slipped from view, the doors clicked shut, insulating us perfectly from the heat and roar. Most poems do not have such a sense of closure.

## Exercise 22:  Meditations on Objects

### Urn Burial

"To live indeed, is to be again ourselves . . . "

Sir Thomas Browne
1605-1682
*Hydriotaphia, Urn-Burial*
1658

### 1.  Still Life with Cracked Urn

". . . the wisdom of funeral laws found the folly of prodigal blazes, and reduced undoing fires unto the rule of sober obsequies, wherein few could be so mean as not to provide wood, pitch, a mourner, and an urn."

*Urn-Burial*

The urn has a Mexican air,
the kind of pot you might display.
Not quite teal, blue tinged with grey,
terra cotta geometric frieze –
two fat bands, two thin,
rectangles between.

I'm wrong. The urn is vaguely Greek.

I lugged it in a knapsack on the plane.
Across the Pacific weak flesh gave in
under the carry-ons' weight.
I padded the urn with guilt,
checked it in a suitcase,
knew it would not survive intact.

Yes, I regret the crack.
Do patterns always have to repeat themselves?

The crack in the lid's thin as a paper cut.
It doesn't mar the base's geometry.
Guests wouldn't see, glancing at this vase,
this lamp manqué, this cookie jar, folk art.

I had faith that glue might work miracles.
The job is quite professional,
yet underneath the lid two gaps remain.
I know them like a tongue.

Nothing will leak – it's not a question of that.
Not ashes, not the soul,
not my memories.

But this urn, lit on a shelf,
tasteful among the funeral home's range –
frigid marble, hussy brass,
fake Ming, garish chrome –
was my last purchase for you,
a gift only I could select.

I wanted something finally to be perfect.


2.  The Circle

The circle shuts up all,
this shape meant to define
what it means to be mortal.
Then follow the infinite line.

## 3. Conservation

Who lives in this open-ended art?
Tangents like roots shoot into the clouds,
breaking the floor of heaven,
or burrow down, anchoring the past.

No mercy in perfection.
Let's have disruption – of a sort –
a chorus of those voices I can summon
who all need mercy.

Give us this day our daily truth
that changes with the centuries.
Oaks last no more than gravestones
now we're poisoning the planet.
Stone crumbles, trunks rot;
animate, inanimate waste alike.

My mother and I live here,
but we'll both be yellow in forty years,
given the paper's weight.

Perhaps I'm addicted to questions as well as patterns.
Like a donkey sniffing a carrot on a stick,
I'm after that line of thought
I can bend just a bit.

I write this now with my favourite pen.
Thomas Browne was my age
when he mused on burials and urns.
Be grateful for small gifts.
Synchronicity again.

## Exercise 23: Response to Legal Jargon

## My Mother's Will

Lawyers arbitrate life's hereafters.
Their prose ripples like a stream
pushing a waterwheel –
a low-tech simile for a will
as unoriginal as what it means:
whereas, wherefore, whereby, bequeath.

Here feeling is invisible
unlike the lawyers' bill
that clutches the heart like a fatal attack.
Where is "mother" in this?
The democratic "decedent" fits all.

      Memories cut like paper,
      refuse to heal.

She avoided tax scams, fancy trusts,
the word "estate" only whispered,
a skeleton in the closet
rattling her thoughts.

Here she is at last,
pressed between documents,
finally thin in perpetuity,
yet she escapes me.

For the moment.

## Exercise 24:  Souvenirs

### Hair

1

Odd how we spend time arranging hair –
dead tissue, outgrowths of the skin –
shining like a beacon, sexual attraction,
these keratins, these proteins,
swinging in the air.

The movie queen's dyed tresses,
clean bob of the athletic,
rock star's unwashed dreads,
shy pageboy, wild punk,
cool Grace Kelly knot,
fifties' crew, Beatles' mop.
Hair merited a musical,
it grew and turned political.

Even a basic cut
tells the world who we think we are.

2

Your hair lies in a silver box,
an ornate Indian heart.
A white-green stone blurred like the earth
from space is fixed in the top.
Locks clipped at the funeral home
nestle in purple plush –
antique silver, coarse as in life.

You always brushed up well.
Shampoo and dryer did the trick.
No gel, no set.

Why collect these strands of skin?

They cannot die, being dead already.
Here silver lies in silver,
tarnished but still shining
in a sympathetic light,
lasting as a thread of memory.

# Exercise 25:  Coda

## Once there was . . . How it Is

"how it was I quote before Pim with Pim after Pim how it is
three parts I say it as I hear it . . .

my life last state last version ill-said ill-heard ill-recaptured
ill-murmured in the mud brief movements of the lower face
losses everywhere"

Samuel Beckett, *How It Is*

Once there was an old woman who lived alone and then didn't.
Not since she finally found a boy friend – the ultimate status
symbol of the elderly widow. They were in love. She had found
love again at last. For the first time, she thought, after thirty-eight
years of marriage.

At first everything was perfect. Mills and Boon for the eighty
plus set. She could talk on the phone without bitterness lingering
in her daughters' ears like tinnitus, a buzz of other agendas. Her
voice rang clear and true like a child soprano's. She was content at
last. For the first time.

This story cannot have a happy ending. All stories must end at
the end as Oedipus knew, solving the Sphinx's riddle that led to
his ascension as king. Human beings rise and fall: they crawl, walk
upright and then limp till they crawl again.

Sunsets fade, even as we ride towards them on those perfectly
bred, sweaty horses, even when we lose sight of our audience. The
horses tire, they go lame, they are shot. We were silly enough to let
happiness go to our heads and headed straight up into the hills.
Night – even a perfect velvet – covers our sadness and we lie alone
under the rocky eaves, shivering with our memories.

That's all right. It's how it is with everyone. We don't have to feel picked on by abstract fate. Some never have the chance to curl up at last with a nice dream that bears some resemblance to reality, warming our insides like a hot cup of tea.

Before her bizarre logic and mood swings exhausted this less than tolerant boyfriend, they had a good canter on the plain. That's how it is at their age, at our age, how it was for her anyway. And probably was for him again for a while, with his new widow after my mother's death.

Yet he kept the wedding ring of my mother's dead husband, my father, which she had given him at first. To bless their unwedded bliss. A souvenir. The last.

If I remember it rightly, if I remember them rightly, at first, when he first met her, at last, when he left. Now or when I'm eighty-seven, her age when she died.

The last time I saw her she asked, "Do you really recall who I was?"